THE DEVILS OF PEGASUS

Bénouville Bridge
June 6th 1944

Author of stories, poetry, teenage and adult fiction, winner of several awards, but also a songwriter, **Patrick Bousquet-Schneeweis** splits his time between Hendaye and Paris. His passion for the history of the two world wars is matched only by his passion for cats. Patrick has happily turned his pen to comic books, working alongside Régis Hector to create comics in the *Les aventures d'Oscar et Mauricette* series.

Other titles by Patrick Bousquet-Schneeweis

- *Héros du Jour J*, Orep.
- *La Balle rouge*, Orep.
- *Bleu chien soleil des tranchées*, Serpenoise.
- *Chance, Les ailes de la liberté*, Serpenoise.
- *Les Neiges de l'enfer*, Serpenoise (Prix jeunesse "Raconte-moi l'Histoire" 2008).
- *Un tank nommé Éternité*, Serpenoise.
- *La Banquise a croqué le Chat noir*, Serpenoise (Prix littéraire des Vosges du jeune lecteur 2006).
- *Shootings*, préfacé par Gilles Perrault, Les 3 Orangers (Prix jeunesse "Raconte-moi l'Histoire" 2012).
- *Félin pour l'autre suivi de Même les souris ont du chagrin*, (co-written with his cat Scot), Les 3 Orangers.

*

Eclectic author, **Michel Giard** has published close to fifty books, the majority of which take maritime history and Normandy as their subject matter. Historian, speaker, globetrotter, reporter for local French radio, Orep Éditions has already published *Phares et feux de Normandie* and *Chansons normandes* by the author.

Other titles by Michel Giard

- *Chansons normandes, du Cotentin à la plaine de Caen*, Orep.
- *Phares et feux de Normandie*, Orep.
- *Les Bateaux du Jour J*, éditions Sutton.
- *Le Carnet de cuisine du Cotentin*, Le Télégramme.
- *Le Dictionnaire du Cotentin*, Le Télégramme.
- *Les Mousses, de Colbert à nos jours*, Le Télégramme.
- *Prendre pied, tenir ou mourir*, Éditions P. Galodé.
- *Les Grandes Catastrophes maritimes du XXe siècle*, Éditions P. Galodé.
- *La Carriole*, Éditions Isoète.

Patrick Bousquet-Schneeweis & Michel Giard

THE DEVILS OF PEGASUS

Bénouville Bridge
June 6th 1944

OREP
EDITIONS

OREP
EDITIONS

Zone tertiaire de Nonant – 14400 BAYEUX
Tel: 02 31 51 81 31 – **Fax:** 02 31 51 81 32
info@orepeditions.com – www.orepeditions.com

Editor: Grégory PIQUE
Conception design: Éditions OREP
Graphics and layout: Sophie YOUF
Editorial coordination: Corine DESPREZ
English translation: Claire SCAMMELL/Mélanie CHANAT

*For Ginette and Emmanuel Gordon,
with love.*
P. B-S.

*For Marcel Legendre, who served in the
Free French Naval Forces and was on board the
Montcalm cruiser on the 6th of June 1944.*
M. G.

Foreword

This text, which has been carefully researched, is a work of fiction.

The authors.

Acknowledgements

Thank you to Béatrice Boissée from the Pegasus Memorial for her insightful comments during the editing of this book.

The promise

Southern England, July 1940.
At the controls of his Spitfire[1], above the White Cliffs of Dover, Flying Officer[2] James Hudson was on the lookout for a Heinkel 111[3] escorted by several Messerschmitt 109s[4] which had been picked up on one of the many radars installed along the coastline.
Twenty minutes earlier, Hudson had performed an emergency take-off from the Tangmere aerodrome in Sussex.
The take-off was so quick that at the moment of the *scramble*[5], he had forgotten to slip the little teddy bear his fiancée Lucy had given him two weeks earlier, on his twentieth birthday, into his jacket pocket.
Hudson took his little mascot on every mission and had developed the habit of kissing the

---

1. One of the most famous British fighter planes used in the Battle of Britain.
2. Equivalent in rank to an Army lieutenant.
3. German bomber.
4. Or Me-109, German fighter plane.
5. Order to take-off immediately.

bear quickly on the nose at the moment of engaging an enemy aircraft.

That morning the sky was clear, there was not a cloud in sight and the sun was shining brightly. Ideal weather for shooting down Huns[6], thought Hudson, initiating a light turn to the left.

He was accompanied by three other Spitfires piloted by new recruits without much *dog-fight*[7] experience.

As a precaution, he had asked them to shadow him and copy his manoeuvres.

Hudson's attention was diverted momentarily by the sight of a fishing boat anchored in a sandy cove. Images of peaceful family holidays flooded his memory; it seemed like another lifetime... another world.

His daydream was suddenly interrupted by an anxious voice yelling in his headphones:

'James! Disengage! Disengage! Bandit[8] at 2 o'clock![9] And you've got another one on your tail!'

---

6. Name given to the Germans by British pilots.
7. Air combat.
8. Name given to Germans pilots by British pilots
9. The position of enemy aircraft is given as a position on a clock face. For example, 12 o'clock means straight ahead, 2 o'clock means to the right.

Hudson thought he recognised the voice of young Harry MacDonald, a Glaswegian who had recently joined Squadron 601.

Taking a quick look to his right, Hudson attempted to straighten up his aircraft.

Too late! He had just received a direct hit from the Me-109's fire.

Hudson felt his Spitfire nose up suddenly under the impact of the bullets, at the same time his windshield was suddenly obscured by a smear of glycol.

He tried a different manoeuvre to disengage. In vain.

The German, feeling Hudson at his mercy, was still on his tail.

The second burst of fire from the Me-109, shorter but just as precise, pierced the cockpit of the Spitfire to hit the British pilot square on the chest.

The last thing James Hudson saw was a young girl sitting at the water's edge, shielding her eyes with her hand, watching the Spitfire tumbling towards the grey waters of the English Channel.

His last thought, as the first flames reached the pockets of his flying suit, was of Lucy.

*

London, two days later.

Chris Hudson was rereading *The Hound of the Baskervilles*, one of his favourite Sherlock Holmes adventures, when the doorbell rang at the modest Whitechapel flat where the young man lived with his parents.

A few moments later he heard his mother sobbing. Chris put down his book and rushed into the living room.
'James was shot down by the *Fritz*,'[10] was all his father said to him, his voice blank as he held him gently in his arms. 'His plane crashed into the Channel. The few witnesses on the scene didn't see a parachute open.'
'My boy! My poor little boy!' cried Mrs Hudson over and over again, the letter which had delivered the terrible news shaking violently in her hands with every sob.

Chris, too distraught to express his grief in words, silently stroked his mother's face and concentrated on fighting back the torrent of tears he felt welling up inside.
He returned to his room hurriedly.
A while later, just 15 years of age, seeing a photo of James in his Royal Air Force uniform, Chris

---
10. Pejorative name given to Germans.

swore to make the *Krauts*[11] pay dearly for his brother's death.
A brother he loved and was so very proud of.

*

Four years went by...

---

[11]. Pejorative name given to Germans.

Normandy objective

Southern England, 5th of June 1944.

Sat on the grass of the huge airfield amid infantrymen, pilots, mechanics, supply trucks, ambulances, ammunition resupply vehicles, bombers and gliders, a solitary soldier with an innocent face and thick, black hair was sharpening his dagger with unhidden joy.
'Oi, Chris, put your Fairbairn[12] away and come and pose for the photo!' shouted a Red Beret with a shaved head and mocking smile.
'Photo? What photo?'
'The one we're having taken with our friend Pegasus!' added the soldier, waving a little soft-toy horse to which a mischievous para had stuck two tiny white cardboard wings. 'You hadn't forgotten that Pegasus is the symbol of the 6th British Airborne Division and that our regiment belongs to that division had you?'

---
12. British commando dagger.

'Okay lads, I'm coming,' replied Hudson, putting his dagger back into its sheath.

A few seconds later, he joined the members of his stick[13] who, in a few hours, were going to be taking part in one of the biggest military operations of all time.

An operation known by the code name Overlord[14].

*

After the death of his brother and long before joining the 6th Airborne Division, Chris had closely followed the series of Allied attempts to invade Adolf Hitler's 'Fortress Europe'.

When the first landing attempt was made by Canadian troops in Dieppe in August 1942 he had listened to the BBC day and night. And he had cried with rage to learn that not only had this operation ended in heavy defeat, many soldiers had lost their lives in the fiasco.

Later, a long while later, Chris had practically jumped for joy when he heard via Jimmy Preston, a school friend who was serving as the driver to an Engineer officer, that plans for another landing operation on the French coast

---
13. Group of paratroopers who jump out of the same plane.
14. See glossary.

had been agreed at the Quebec conference in 1943.

The only extra bit of detail Hudson had managed to glean was that the operation would take place at some point in 1944.
A few days later, soon after his nineteenth birthday, and to the great distress of his parents who had already lost one son to this war, Chris enlisted as a paratrooper.

*

Chris Hudson was now a member of D company *2nd Ox & Bucks* commanded by Major John Howard.
The men's mission – a mission they learnt about at the beginning of May 1944 – was to take the Bénouville and Ranville bridges located between Caen and the sea.
It was essential to take the bridges intact because they would provide the only passage between the *Sword Beach* sector where the British were to land and the bridgehead.

The assault by the 6th Airborne Division was planned for the night before the landings.
According to intelligence held by Allied headquarters, these bridges were being guarded by fifty or so well armed German soldiers.

Once the bridges had been taken, and if everything went as planned, Major Howard's commandos would be joined by Lord Lovat's men the next day; they were due to land close to Ouistreham at around 7:30 in the morning. 'Holding for almost 12 hours against the Fritz, not to mention resisting a possible counter-attack, it's a heck of a gamble,' muttered Peter Watson in Chris' ear as they were being told the details of their mission.

'You're right, but this is exactly the kind of challenge I like,' replied Hudson, smiling. A moment later he tapped Peter on the shoulder, raising his eyes to the sky, 'Besides, it's out of our hands, isn't it?' he added fatalistically.

In order to prepare his men, Major Howard had erected a large and very realistic model using details provided by the French Resistance. Better yet, near the city of Exeter in Devon there was a site very similar to the location of the two bridges. The assault was rehearsed here, over and over again, for six days straight.

*

Hudson, together with the other paras taking part in the operation, was awaiting the order to board the Horsa[15] gliders which would take them to their target.

They were becoming all the more impatient to leave since the landings had already been delayed by one day as a result of the awful weather over the Channel at this time of the year.

After consulting with the weather experts for a final time, General Eisenhower, commander of the Allied forces, had given the green light a few hours earlier.

The beach landings would finally take place at dawn on the 6th of June.

The men of the 6th Airborne Division, who in a few hours would be climbing into their gliders, would be among the first to enter the battle.

Chris didn't yet know that he would soon meet a certain Bill Millin, the piper[16] appointed to Lord Lovat's commando...

---

15. See glossary.
16. Bagpipes player.

Bill Millin

Near Southampton, the piper Bill Millin was about to board a landing craft along with the men of the *1st Special Service Brigade*, under the command of Lord Lovat.

Fate had plans for Bill Millin; he was about to become a part of Normandy landings history.

Scottish by blood, he was born in Canada in 1922. A member of Clan McMillin, with connections to Clan Cameron, he had completed his commando training in the Highlands, at Achnacarry to be precise.

Well-liked by his fellow commandos thanks to his remarkable bagpipe playing, Millin, soon before operation Overlord was set in motion, and, it has to be said, to his great surprise, was chosen by Lord Lovat to become the piper attached to the *1st Special Service Brigade*.

On the 6th of June he would be landing on *Sword Beach* and accompanying Lovat's men with the sound of his instrument to Bénouville Bridge where they were due to effect a junction with John Howard's men.

*

At present, Bill Millin was crossing a wooden footbridge over a small but fast-flowing river.
With a heavy heart, walking in driving rain, Bill was on his way back from visiting his fiancée Fiona, whom he had just told about his coming departure for Southern England where the Allied armada were gathering.
When would he see his fiancée again? He didn't know.
Would he ever see her again?
And would he ever again see this landscape of heather fields in the shadows of snow-capped Ben Nevis?
Nothing was certain.

In an attempt to overcome the melancholy he felt gradually building up inside, Millin thought of Fiona again and of their last romantic walk in this stunning landscape that he never tired of. To give him courage, he also thought of all the happy tunes he would play for his fellow commandos to celebrate his departure.

Having very quickly regained his good mood, Bill Millin followed the path to camp Achnacarry with a determined stride.

Before the assault

Harwell RAF Base. Night of the 5th – 6th of June 1944.

'What are you up to?' a jolly-faced Red Beret asked Chris.
'I'm writing to my parents, you never know what might happen, eh?'
'You're not wrong. I just now sent my girl one last card myself. Look', added the soldier proudly, producing a photo of a young blonde girl with big, smiling eyes from his jacket. 'She's gorgeous isn't she, my Cheryl?'
'Wow! You're a lucky man to have a fiancée like that. I wish the same could be said for me! But it's my own fault, maybe I have trouble committing or maybe I enjoy my freedom too much, who knows?! Okay, leave me alone now, I've got to read over my letter to make sure I haven't made too many mistakes. My dad is an English teacher you see, it wouldn't look good! What's your name anyway?'
'Crabbtree. Francis Crabbtree. I think we're in the same stick'.

'Pleased to meet you. I'm Hudson. Chris Hudson'.

'Well then, see you later, Chris!' said Crabbtree, gesturing to the Horsa gliders parked behind the Halifax bombers which would soon be taking them across the Channel.

Turning away from his new friend, Hudson read out his letter quietly to himself:

"Southern England, 5th of June 1944.

Dearest Mum and Dad,

These few lines were written just before boarding the glider which is going to take me to our mission, to reassure you I'm okay.
This is it! We're going! Ike[17] *has finally given the green light!*
Know that I am very proud to be taking part in this huge operation which, I hope, will annihilate a large amount of Hitler's troops and his circle of degenerates.
I'll be thinking of you in the thick of battle of course, but also of James, my dear brother, whose tragic fate I have never been able to forget.
I leave you now to go and collect my "invasion money" from the paymasters and my English-French

---

17. Eisenhower's nickname.

and English-German conversation booklets.

I'm sending you all my love and hoping to send you more good news very soon.

Chris

P.S: Dad, even though you don't really believe, please pray for me over the coming days. It can only help... Thank you!"

Then, no doubt for fear of getting too emotional, Hudson quickly sealed his letter. A few moments later he deposited it in a large mail sack, already filled to the brim, which had been set up in the mail officer's tent.

*

It was just before 11pm when Hudson and his fellow commandos headed in silence towards Horsa glider No.1 in which Major John Howard himself had just taken his seat.
The emotion which gripped the paratroopers was almost palpable. Every one of them, at that very moment, was all too conscious of the importance of their mission. Conscious of the incalculable consequences that the mission's

failure would have on the success of Operation Overlord[18].

Chris let out a quiet satisfied sigh when he saw *Staff Sergeant*[19] Jim Wallwork at the controls. His reputation as a pilot was firmly established.

Just as he had done with every para as they boarded the glider overloaded with kit, Wallwork greeted Chris with a friendly wave.

Hudson sat down next to someone he didn't recognise, their face blackened with burnt cork. He took a few seconds to realise the face belonged to Francis Crabbtree.

'Well I never! You've certainly made an effort to go unnoticed!' laughed Hudson.
'I knew you'd like it!' joked Crabbtree. 'You don't look too bad yourself, Chris! You could pass for a veritable chimney sweep!'

Take-off was imminent; the engines of the Halifax bombers could be heard turning.

'We're off!' announced Lieutenant Den Brotheridge a few moments later, feeling the cable connecting the Horsa to the four-engined plane tighten suddenly. 'Good luck

---
18. See glossary.
19. Non-commissioned officer equivalent to a corporal.

everyone! And don't forget lads, the only good Nazi is a dead Nazi!'

'Don't you worry,' murmured Chris under his breath, 'I'll remember, you can count on me'.

The target

No one on board glider No.1 said a word.
Every man was shut away in a bubble of silence, thinking either about his family, the dreadful battles ahead or what he would do afterwards, when Nazi Germany finally lost the war.
If he was lucky enough to see that day.

The calm was soon interrupted by the cheery voice of the co-pilot, clearly hoping to lighten the mood a little:
'In less than a minute we will be crossing the Channel! Anyone who wants to swim please put on your bathing suits now!'
One nervous laugh from the back of the aircraft was his only response.
'You okay?' Hudson asked Crabbtree a bit later, who was whistling quietly.
'Yeah. I just hope that the German fighters aren't out tonight. It would be a shame to go down without even having fought!'
'You're right. But, in my opinion, what we should be most afraid of is the *Flak*[20], which

---
20. German anti-aircraft defence.

will no doubt be unleashed the minute we're over French soil'.

Almost at that very moment, the first round of gunfire could be heard in the distance.

'What was I just saying?' said Chris, clasping his hands together nervously. 'I don't reckon we're very far from the coast'.

*

The sky was being lit up by the criss-cross of searchlights and flares tracing the path of the bombers and gliders, while heavy fire accompanied by countless little black flecks was getting closer all the time.

Luckily, none of the shells or tracer bullets reached their target.

It was gone midnight when the three gliders tasked with taking Bénouville Bridge were released from their tow-planes.

'It feels good to be flying solo!' said one para to another sat to the left of Crabbtree as glider No.1 plunged faster and faster towards the ground.

*

Gefreiter[21] Klaus Wolf looked at his watch again.

In five minutes it would be midnight, time for him to meet Anne-Marie in an abandoned barn near Café Gondrée[22], which was just on the other side of the bridge, opposite Café Picot.

Wolf was thrilled to be meeting up with the young and pretty Normandy girl he had hit it off with two days earlier.

That morning two days ago, Wolf had gone to Monsieur and Madame Colin's farm for milk, eggs and butter, while he was there he encountered their maid; their eyes met.

He had fallen for her immediately.

The soldier's great presence and good manners must have worked their charm on Anne too since she had agreed to meet him on the night of the 5th – 6th for what he discreetly described as 'a little stroll' in the surrounding countryside.

Having given his hair one last comb, Wolf was just about to set off for the barn when he heard what sounded like an enormous gust of wind to his right, coming from the sky.

Looking up, he could make out three aircraft

---

21. Rank equivalent to a corporal.
22. Famous café on the west side of Pegasus Bridge which has become a must-visit establishment for tourists and D-Day veterans.

fast approaching the bridge. Wolf saw the roundels and white bands painted on the sides of the aircraft and knew immediately that he wouldn't be seeing Anne-Marie that night after all.

Running as fast as his legs would carry him, he headed for the bunker where he had left his submachine gun, shouting to the rest of his unit who were yet unaware of the invasion: '*Alarm! Alarm!*'

*

With the glider doors now open, Howard's men could make out rows of hedges marking out fields, orchards, meadows and the silver-coloured ribbons of the Caen canal and the Orne River.

Their eyes searched desperately for anti-aircraft poles, possibly mined, which, according to intelligence, the Germans had set up and on which the Horsas were in danger of becoming impaled.

In glider No.1, under the command of Lieutenant Brotheridge, the Red Berets were braced arm-in-arm ready for the huge impact of the aircraft hitting the ground.

Soon after, there was a deafening noise and the Horsa, skidding like a temperamental horse, furrowed the ground in a shower of sparks before coming to a stop near the barbed wire surrounding the bridge.

The violent landing left some of the soldiers stunned, but they came round after a few seconds.

'Everyone out! Move it lads!' yelled an officer as he leapt out of the aircraft, his Sten[23] in his hand.

That's when all hell broke loose...

---

23. British submachine gun.

Ham and jam!

Submachine gun in hand, Chris was one of the first to extricate himself from the wreckage of the glider.

Spotting a figure about ten metres off wearing an easily recognisable helmet, Hudson opened fire in his direction.

Hit square on the chest, the German did a pirouette before collapsing heavily on the bridge.

Very quickly, the men from gliders No.2 and No.3 joined Lieutenant Brotheridge and his men.

Spotting an enemy soldier taking his gun out of its holster to fire a flare alarm, Brotheridge killed him instantly.

'Find the explosive charges underneath the bridge and destroy them before the Fritz have a chance to blow everything up!' ordered the officer before charging towards the other bank, followed by Hudson and Crabbtree.

A few moments later, the British officer, hit on the throat by a bullet, was the next to fall.

'Brotheridge is hit!' cried Hudson furiously

to the men as he continued his crazy course through gunfire and exploding grenades. 'Show no mercy, lads!'

Near a flaming sentry box, a German emerging from a trench with his hands raised in surrender was also shot down immediately. The attackers had now reached the other side of the bridge.

Grenade explosions, gunshots and submachine fire were continuous.

Little by little however, they saw the German resistance weaken.

From the refuge of small bunkers, the last of the defence either managed to flee or were quickly taken out of action.

Stunned from the explosion of a phosphorous grenade at the start of the battle, *Gefreiter* Klaus Wolf had taken refuge behind an embankment, from where he could follow the battle.

During a moment of confusion and under the cover of a thick cloud of smoke, he managed to leave his shelter without being noticed.

*

As the lifeless body of Lieutenant Brotheridge was being recovered, a para approached Lance Corporal Edward Tappenden and ordered him:

'Ranville Bridge has just been taken too! It's time! Send the signal!'
Tappenden was only too willing to accept this order, he brought the radio's microphone to his lips and relayed the coded message announcing the success of their mission:
'Ham and jam, ham and jam! I repeat, *ham and jam!'*

One of the first D-Day battles was over. It had barely lasted twenty minutes.

A short while later, when the majority of the men of the 6th Airborne Division were congratulating one another and celebrating their victory, they were interrupted suddenly by an emotional and tired voice:
'Hey, don't celebrate too soon, lads. The hardest part is still to come. Now we have to hold the bridges while we wait for reinforcements.'

There was a long and anxious night ahead...

Sword Beach

6th of June 1944, 7:25am.

On board the *LCI 501*[24] which had left England the day before, the piper Bill Millin could not believe his eyes.
All around him, the sea was covered in boats of all sorts and sizes, from battleships to minesweepers.
Emerging from the mist like a huge ghostly armada, the ships had one by one taken up position in front of *Sword Beach*, one of the British landing sectors.
At the same time, hundreds of aircraft, bombers and fighter planes, attacked the blockhouses and fortifications which were defending the beach, but also road and railway communication routes.
In front of him, Bill could barely make out the coast, concealed by thick smoke, at which battleships, cruisers and destroyers were shooting continuously.

---

24. Landing Craft Infantry.

'What's the matter with them, the *Fritz*? said a Royal Marines commando, straightening up his beret. 'If this carries on, with a bit of luck, we won't even need to fight!'
'Don't be so sure, old boy!' replied Millin, fighting back the hiccups that had come with the sea sickness which had kept him awake most of the night. 'Those bleeding Krauts, they'll have enough left to take us down for a while yet, believe you me. I've got one piece of advice: watch your back!'
As if to illustrate his point, at that very moment a shell was fired from a villa-turned-bunker and exploded not far from them, sending up an enormous geyser of foamy seawater.

The *LCI 501* was barely a hundred metres from the beach now.
A beach already littered with various obstacles including the wreckage of burnt tanks and other vehicles. It was the moment that Lord Lovat chose to jump off the boat
Bill Millin followed him immediately, lifting his bagpipes over his head to keep them dry. A few moments later, he started to play "*Highland Ladies*" – a tune which Lovat seemed to particularly enjoy – against the roar of explosions and automatic weapon fire which swept through the entire area.

Millin then moved on to "*The Road To The Isles*", pacing up and down the sand all the while, to the amazement of a number of soldiers, who took him for a madman, if not a raving lunatic.
Then, spotting Lord Lovat talking with an officer behind a dune, Millin ran over to join him.

All the while, the landed troops, in spite of the losses they had suffered, had continued bravely advancing on the beach.
Turning around, Millin surveyed the scene; tears came to his eyes to see the tragedy being played out before him.
The beach was already scattered with bodies. They would soon be joined by dozens more brought in by the tide.
Behind an anti-tank wall or sheltered by a dune, overwhelmed doctors were giving initial treatment to soldiers with injuries of varying severity. A bit further along, near a network of chevaux-de-frise[25] and barbed wire fencing, a Crab[26] tank was almost completely burnt out.

Soon after, on Lord Lovat's signal, and keeping an eye out for mines and snipers, the men

---

25. A portable defensive barrier, usually covered with barbed wire.
26. A tank with a rotating roller on the front with chains attached to it which would hit the ground causing mines to explode.

stood up from their crouched positions and started to advance inland.

'Hey, Piper, aren't you going to play us something to give us courage?' yelled a French commando to Millin, his uniform covered in blood and dirt.

Millin didn't need to be asked twice.

And it was to the sound of his bagpipes that the soldiers set off with the hope of joining, very soon, John Howard and his men, who had been holding the Bénouville and Ranville bridges for several hours now...

The junction

Crouched in rapidly dug out trenches, or hiding in shelters taken from the Germans during their assault, the soldiers of the 6th Airborne Division were exhausted. They had sustained mortar fire and isolated gunshots for most of the night, impatiently waiting for dawn to break. The men's faces were gaunt with fatigue and tension, not to mention the grief of losing some of their best men, including Lieutenant Brotheridge. All morning they had faced a series of enemy attempts to regain the bridges linking the Caen Canal and the River Orne. However, so far, the British had succeeded in resisting their attackers...

*

'What's that awful smell?' asked Crabbtree, pinching his nose and grimacing in disgust.
'It must be the carcass of a cow or horse blown up by a mine,' replied Hudson. 'There is a farm not far from here. But you're right, it stinks!

Those poor animals, they too are paying a heavy toll for this damned war!'

'Do you reckon reinforcements will arrive soon?' asked Crabbtree, checking the cartridge clip on his Bren machine gun again.

'I hope so, because we won't be able to hold much longer. Some of our lads are starting to run out of ammunition. I overheard Corporal Everton earlier talking about an imminent enemy counter-attack with Tiger[27] or Panther[28] tanks! If it's true, we don't stand a chance!'

'Don't talk it up!' yelled a Red Beret crouched in a shell hole not far from them. 'Especially since we don't have much to stop or destroy them... Apart from a few PIAT[29], if that...'

Now Hudson was worried, 'Maybe the invasion forces were driven back into the sea!' he said, looking nervously at his watch. 'If that's the case...'

'Calm down, Chris!' said Crabbtree. 'Here, take this chocolate bar. I found it on the Fritz

---
27. See glossary.
28. See glossary.
29. See glossary.

I took out earlier as he was about to cross the canal. Perhaps that will get your spirits up!'
'Thanks! I could use it!'

At that very moment, a bullet came out of nowhere and whistled past his ears.

'That bloody sniper! swore Hudson ducking his head. 'I haven't figured out his location yet, but if I ever get hold of him, he's in for a pretty nasty quarter of an hour, believe you me! He's been shooting at us long enough!'

*

It was around midday when Chris thought he could make out a sound that didn't really belong on the battlefield.

'What are you... ?' started Crabbtree.

'Shut up! Listen! Can't you hear it? I can hear something like music in the distance...'

Crabbtree listened carefully in the relative quiet between heavy machine gun fire and the launch of a mortar shell close by.

'You're right! It sounds like... Yes, it is! That's the sound of bagpipes!'

'It's Lovat and his commandos, I'm sure of it!' exclaimed Chris, overjoyed. 'Lovat is coming!' he cried all around, his helmet swinging side to side. 'We're saved, lads!'

'They're only an hour and a half late!' remarked one of the men, his uniform torn in places. 'But,' he added with a laugh, 'I don't think we'll hold it against them eh, fellas?'

*

'Piper!' called Lord Lovat to Bill Millin almost at that very same moment, who was calmly blowing into his bagpipes in the midst of automatic weapon fire. 'In a few minutes we are going to effect the junction with the paras. Carry on playing "*Blue Bonnets Over The Border*". Understood? And for as long as you can! I'm counting on you!'

'Yes, sir! replied Millin. 'And if you don't mind, later on, when we're on the Ranville Bridge, I will move on to "*The March of the Cameron Men*".'

'Perfect!'

Without losing his calm, Bill Millin took hold of his loyal bagpipes again. And, as if he were standing on the edge of a loch in his dear Scotland, he resumed playing to the cheers of a few locals who, braving the danger, had ventured onto the battlefield outside of their homes to greet and offer flowers to their liberators.

The farm of death

A bit later that afternoon...

'Hello Piper,' said Chris as he approached Bill Millin sat under the remains of an apple tree. 'Tell me, is playing the bagpipes complicated? I've always dreamed of owning a set!'

Millin replied with a smile, while swotting away the swarm of aggressive mosquitoes swirling around him:

'It takes a few years to learn, of course, but also a decent pair of lungs and a good repertoire! Not to mention a relentless desire to please, or,' he added with a laugh, 'to offend the ears of a less enthusiastic audience! If you like, I can show you how it works, once the sector has calmed down a bit. You will find me in one of the trenches near the ruined farm that you can see to your left. We'll share the bottle of cider that a local farmer gave me this morning and think sweet thoughts of the motherland and the girls back home.

'I look forward to it, Bill,' said Hudson, shaking his hand warmly. 'So, see you this evening perhaps'.

*

Since the attack on the Bénouville Bridge, in which most of the men in his unit had died or been taken prisoner, *Gefreiter* Klaus Wolf had taken refuge in the remains of a farm at least two hundred metres from the British positions. The main building had been destroyed by a bomb dropped by a B-17[30] three weeks earlier, and its inhabitants had fled to the home of parents in Alençon.
Wolf was hiding in the loft of barn, or what was left of it. The loft was accessed by a wooden ladder which the German removed after each of his forays into the surrounding area to find something to eat. It was during one of these nightly forays that he took a Walther P38 and a dagger from an SS officer whose decaying body lay behind a burnt-out lorry.

From the dormer window overlooking the surrounding countryside, Wolf could see British and French soldiers, paratroopers and commandos, going about their tasks in

---
30. American bomber nicknamed Flying Fortress.

preparation for continuing the offensive on to Caen. He had thought seriously about giving himself up several times, but the fear that he would be executed without a formal procedure had dissuaded him so far.

To regain his freedom, Wolf was therefore banking on a German counter-attack supported by tanks which, he was certain, was sure to happen at one point or another.

Wolf was deep in these thoughts when he saw the ginger cat which came to visit him from time to time, cautiously enter through the barn door.

The German immediately put the ladder back in place and climbed down quickly to give his little pet something to eat.

*

Chris loved animals, especially cats. He had taken in a stray that he'd found on his street, just after the death of his brother James. It was a black cat with a pretty white face which he named Bluebell. He loved that cat. Its company and affectionate purring helped him to gradually exorcise his grief. That morning, Chris had just dug a new trench which he was fortifying with wooden planks when, looking up suddenly, he noticed a ginger cat sneaking into the nearby farm. Without really knowing why, Hudson put down his shovel and headed toward the building.

A few moments later, just as he was stepping through the barn, his eyes looking around for the cat, he felt a presence behind him.
He wanted to turn around, but suddenly felt a sharp steel point pressing into his back.
Chris just had time to make out his attacker – a blond, portly soldier, wearing a feldgrau[31] uniform – before falling dead onto the straw, rubble and waste-covered ground.

Without wasting any time, Wolf re-sheathed the dagger he had just used to kill this all too curious soldier and decide to leave right away.
He didn't get very far.
As he was navigating his way around a hedge, shrapnel originating from German lines slit his throat, half decapitating him.
The last thing he saw before he died was a ginger cat, terrorised by the shelling, racing away across the fields...

*

Chris Hudson was buried two days later, in the British cemetery in Ranville. His body still

---
31. The grey-green uniform of German soldiers.

rests there today along with more than two thousand of his fellow service men. The men from his unit were greatly surprised to see the piper Bill Millin at the burial, who played "*The Nut Brown Maiden*" with unhidden emotion in honour of the young soldier with whom he had only had a chance to exchange a few words.

Today

Many of the protagonists in this story, who, in the words of those leading the Allied Forces during Operation Overlord, carried out "one of the greatest aerial exploits of the second world war", are no longer with us.
And, sadly, we can be sure that when we come to celebrate the 70th anniversary of the Normandy Landings in 2014, many other veterans will be missing also.

*

General Sir Richard Gale, commander of the 6th Airborne Division, died in 1982. Major John Howard who commanded the assault on Bénouville Bridge, now known as *Pegasus Bridge*, died in 1999.

As for Bill Millin, who accompanied Lord Lovat's commandos with his bagpipes as they advanced from *Sword Beach* to *Pegasus Bridge*, passed away in August 2010. Two months earlier, he had visited Normandy, a place he cherished above all else, for the final time.

For years, tourists, visitors to the *Pegasus Bridge* memorial and customers of the famous Café Gondrée[32] could find Bill Millin here at the site of his exploits. He would play his famous "*Blue Bonnets Over the Border*", pacing up and down as he had done on the 6th of June 1944 on the Bénouville Bridge to the delight of his audience.

In his honour, the *D-Day Piper Bill Millin* Association erected a memorial in Colleville-Montgomery, the town where the famous piper landed. Erected in June 2013, the statue shows him playing his bagpipes dressed as he was on the morning of D-Day, in homage, as was his wish, to all those who fought in Normandy.

---

32. Famous café on the west side of Pegasus Bridge which has become a must-visit establishment for tourists and D-Day veterans.

HISTORICAL BACKGROUND

AIRBORNE

Map of the Battle of Normandy

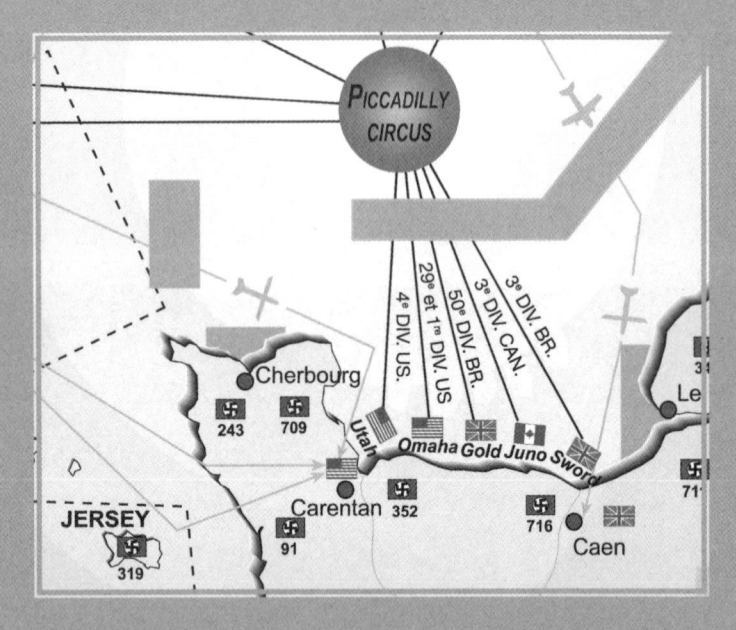

On the 6th of June 1944, at dawn, the Allied invasion fleet appears on the Normandy coast. To the west, American troops of Force "U" land on the beach in La Madeleine in the Utah Beach sector. Force "O" attack the area known as Omaha Beach, which stretches from Vierville-sur-Mer to Sainte-Honorine-des-Pertes. Next along is the British sector, comprising Gold Beach – between Graye-sur-Mer and Arromanches, Juno Beach – between Graye-sur-Mer and Luc-sur-Mer, and Sword Beach – between the mouth of the Orne River in Ouistreham and Lion-sur-Mer. It is at Sword Beach that the 177 French soldiers of Commando Kieffer fight the enemy.

Map of Sword Beach sector and Bénouville Bridge

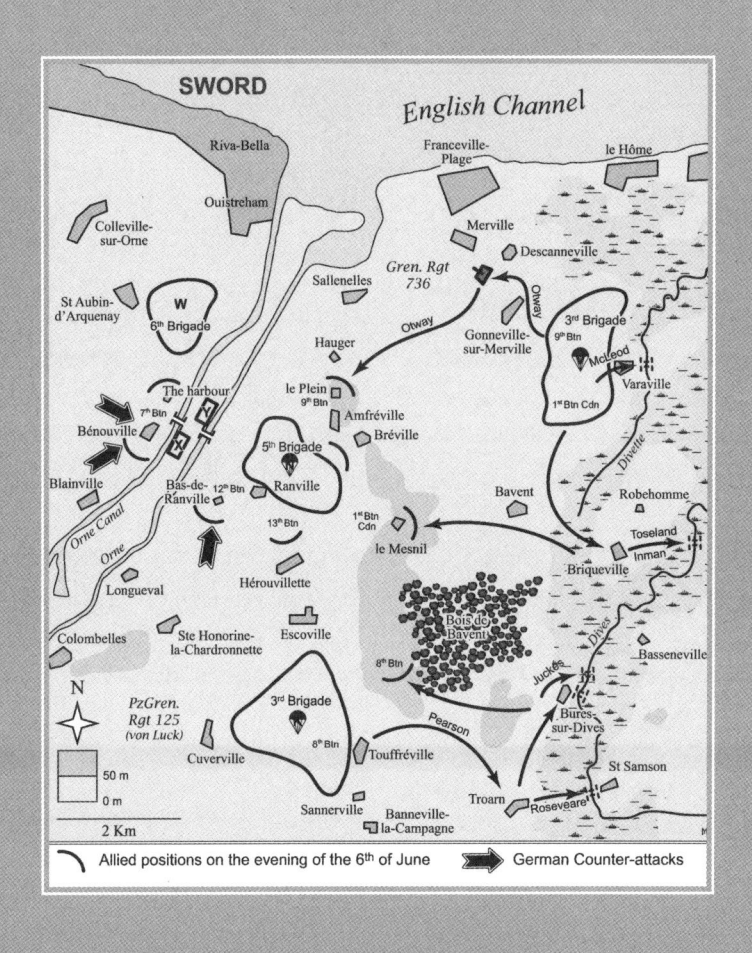

Key figures

Dwight D. EISENHOWER (1890-1969)

Known by his officers as "Ike", Dwight Eisenhower was commander of the Allied Forces in Northern Africa and then in Italy. Following the Tehran Conference, he was appointed Supreme Commander of the Allied Forces in Europe and was responsible for preparations for one of the biggest operations in military history: the Normandy landings. After the war he started a very successful career as a politician and was President of the United States from 1952 to 1960.

John HOWARD (1912-1999)

Enlisted in the army in 1931 aged 19, he was commander of D company of the 6th Airborne Division and took part in the battles of the Battle of France. On the 6th of June 1944 he achieved his objective: take the Bénouville and Ranville bridges and hold them until reinforcements arrive. After the war, he left the army following a serious car accident. He returned to Normandy every year to lay a wreath where he had landed. In the film *The Longest Day*, he was played by Richard Todd, a D-Day paratrooper himself.

Sir Bernard MONTGOMERY (1887-1976)

It was in the sands of the desert, against Field Marshal Rommel, that Montgomery achieved fame by winning the Second Battle of El Alamein. In January 1944 he became Eisenhower's deputy and dedicated his energy to preparations for the landings. He commanded the British troops who were forced to a halt outside Caen by a German blockade for weeks.

Lord LOVAT (1911-1995)

A famous Scot and very much Lord of the Highlands, Simon Christopher Fraser took part in the Dieppe raid on the 19th of August 1942 and then in the Normandy landings as commander of the 1st Special Service Brigade, which was comprised of four units of Royal Marine commandos. He was accompanied by the piper Bill Millin, who played his bagpipes to raise the commandos' spirits. His mission was to relieve Major Howard, who was holding the Bénouville Bridge. On the 8th of May 2014, a statue was erected in his honour at the Kieffer monument in Ouistreham.

Important dates

January 1933: Adolf Hitler takes power.

September 1939: start of the Second World War.

May 1940: invasion of France.

18th of June 1940: General Charles de Gaulle makes his Appeal to the French Resistance.

July to September 1940: battle of Britain.

7th of December 1941: the US enters the war following the Japanese attack on Pearl Harbour.

August 1943: plans for an Allied landing in Normandy are agreed at the Quebec Conference.

6th of June 1944: allied landings in Normandy.

15th of August 1944: allied landings in Provence.

22nd of August 1944: end of the Battle of Normandy.

25th of August 1944: liberation of Paris.

December 1944: the Battle of the Bulge.

30th of April 1945: death of Adolf Hitler in the ruins of Berlin.

8th of May 1945: German surrender.

September 1945: Japan surrenders on the *Missouri* battleship. The Second World War is finally over.

Glossary

Overlord: name given by the Allies to the military operations executed in order to land on the French coast on the 6th of June 1944.

Panther: german tank weighing around forty-five tons.

PIAT (Projector, Infantry, Anti-Tank): british rocket-launcher. Equivalent to the American bazooka or German Panzerfaust.

Horsa glider: the Horsa was the largest assault glider used during the Second World War. In total 3,644 were produced. The Horsa could hold two men in the cockpit as well as twenty-five soldiers with their kit. First used in the invasion of Sicily, the gliders were used mainly in Normandy and then in Holland and Germany. The Horsa gliders were either towed by Halifax, Stirling, Albermarle or Whitley bombers.

Tiger: a fifty-four ton German tank feared by the Allies because of its formidable 88mm gun.

Major Howard's Horsa gliders landed just metres from the bridge. Café Gondrée can be seen behind the trees.

Main museums about the Battle of Normandy

- **Arromanches:** D-Day museum and 360° circular cinema
- **Bayeux:** Memorial museum of the Battle of Normandy
- **Bénouville:** Café Gondrée
- **Caen:** Peace memorial
- **Catz :** Normandy Tank Museum
- **Cherbourg:** Museum of the Liberation
- **Colleville-sur-Mer:** Overlord Museum
- **Courseulles-sur-Mer:** The Juno Beach centre
- **Douvres-la-Délivrande:** Radar museum
- **Falaise:** Août 44 museum
- **Grandcamp-Maisy:** Rangers museum
- **Merville-Franceville:** Museum of the Battle of Merville
- **Montormel:** Museum of the Battle of Normandy
- **Ouistreham Riva-Bella:** No.4 Commando Museum and Museum of the Atlantic Wall, "the Grand Bunker"
- **Quinéville:** Museum of Freedom
- **Ranville:** Pegasus memorial
- **Saint-Côme-du-Mont:** D-Day paratrooper historic centre
- **Saint-Laurent-sur-Mer:** Omaha Beach Memorial museum
- **Sainte-Marie-du-Mont:** Utah Beach D-Day museum
- **Sainte-Mère-Église:** Airborne museum
- **Ver-sur-Mer:** America Gold Beach museum
- **Vierville-sur-Mer:** Omaha D-Day museum

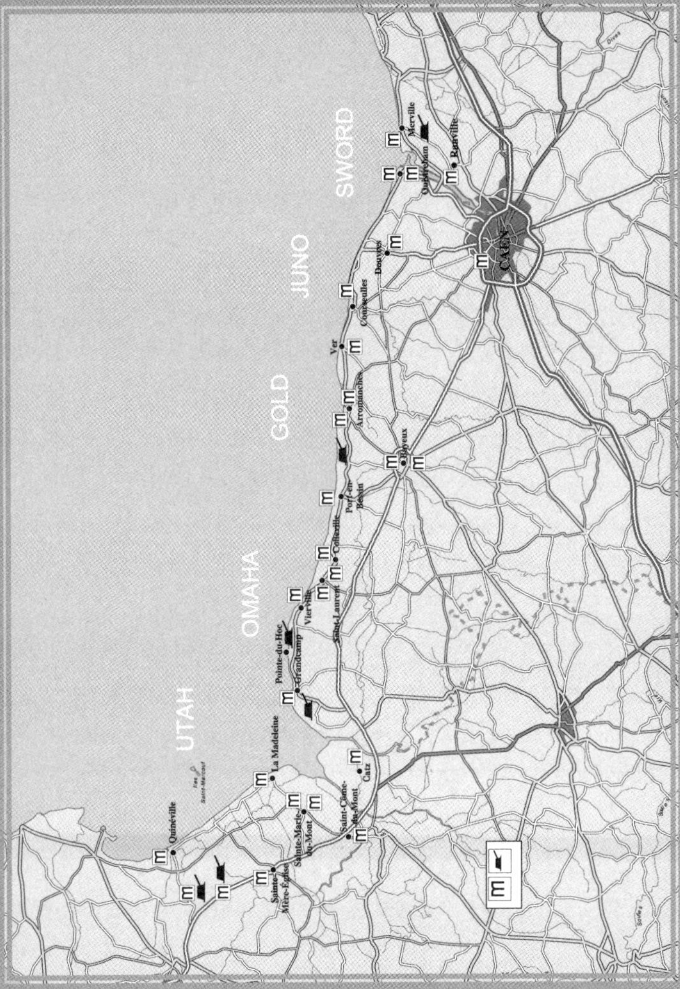
UTAH
OMAHA
GOLD
JUNO
SWORD
CAEN
Quinéville
Sainte-Mère-Église
Sainte-Marie-du-Mont
Saint-Côme-du-Mont
Catz
La Madeleine
Grandcamp
Pointe-du-Hoc
Vierville
Saint-Laurent
Colleville
Port-en-Bessin
Bayeux
Arromanches
Ver
Courseulles
Douvres
Ouistreham
Ranville
Merville

Bibliography

BEEVOR Antony, *D-Day et la bataille de Normandie*, Calmann-Lévy, 2010.

BERNAGE Georges, *Diables Rouges en Normandie*, Éditions Heimdal, 2002.

CARELL Paul, *Ils arrivent*, Laffont, 1962.

COLLIER Richard, *Le jour de l'Aigle*, Presses de la Cité, 1959.

FLORENTIN Eddy, *Stalingrad en Normandie*, Presses de la Cité, 1964.

FLORENTIN Eddy, *Le Guide des plages du débarquement et de la bataille de Normandie*, Perrin.

HOWARTH David, *6 juin à l'aube*, Presses de la Cité, 1959.

JULLIAN Marcel, *La bataille d'Angleterre*, Presses de la Cité, 1965.

MILLIN Bill, *La Cornemuse du D-Day*, Éditions Heimdal, 1994.

PERRAULT Gilles, *Le Grand Jour*, J.-C. Lattès, 1994.

PIPET Albert, *Parachutés sur Sainte-Mère-Église*, Presses de la Cité, 1974.

QUELLIEN Jean, *Les Américains en Normandie*, Orep, 2012.

QUELLIEN Jean, *Normandie 44*, Orep, 2011.

RYAN Cornélius, *Le Jour le plus long*, Laffont, 1960.

Filmography of the Normandy Landings

ESWAY Alexandre, *They are not Angels*, 1947.

FULLER Samuel, *The Big Red One*, 1980.

HANKS Tom, SPIELBERG Steven, *Band of Brothers*, 2001 (10-part mini-series).

MCLAGLEN André Victor, *Breakthrough*, 1978.

PARRISH Robert, *Up from the Beach*, 1965.

SPIELBERG Steven, *Saving Private Ryan*, 1998.

ZANUCK Darryl F., *The Longest Day*, 1962.

British soldiers crossing the bridge after it was taken. Major Howard's gliders can be seen in the background.

Lord Lovat's commandos marching inland to Bénouville Bridge.

67

The statue of piper Bill Millin in Colleville-Montgomery,
work of Gaëtan Ader, published with the courtesy of the artist.

Table of contents

The promise ... 7
Normandy objective ... 13
Bill Millin ... 19
Before the assault ... 23
The target ... 29
Ham and Jam! ... 35
Sword Beach ... 39
The junction ... 43
The farm of death ... 49
Today ... 55

Historical background

Map of the Battle of Normandy ... 58
Map of Sword Beach sector and Bénouville Bridge ... 59
Key figures ... 60
Important dates ... 62
Glossary ... 63
Main museums about the Battle of Normandy ... 64
Bibliography/Filmography of the Normandy Landings ... 66

Dans la même collection

LES ÉRABLES DE SANG
Juno Beach - 6 juin 1944

- Patrick BOUSQUET-SCHNEEWEIS et Michel GIARD
- Format : 130 x 210 mm
- 80 pages intérieures
- Couverture souple
- Dos carré, collé, cousu
- Langues : français, anglais
- Prix : 7,50 €

– Ici Marcel Ouimet de Radio Canada. Je me trouve avec les hommes du régiment de la Chaudière devant une petite station balnéaire nommée Bernières-sur-Mer. Des tirs d'obus en provenance des batteries allemandes s'intensifient autour de nous ! L'ordre de l'assaut est enfin donné ! J'imagine l'émotion de nos valeureux soldats en ces instants historiques car, pour beaucoup, dans leurs veines, coule du sang français...
De Montréal à Juno Beach, l'incroyable odyssée des Canadiens qui, le 6 juin 1944, nous ont aidés à recouvrer notre liberté...

LES FANTÔMES DE PORT-WINSTON
Arromanches - 6 juin 1944

- Patrick BOUSQUET-SCHNEEWEIS et Michel GIARD
- Format : 130 x 210 mm
- 80 pages intérieures
- Couverture souple
- Dos carré, collé, cousu
- Langues : français, anglais
- Prix : 7,50 €

La vision des vestiges des pontons d'Arromanches embua de larmes les yeux de Julie, qui ne put s'empêcher de frissonner. Les spectres, qu'elle avait pensé exorciser en faisant le voyage jusqu'ici, étaient de retour. Plus présents que jamais...
De la construction du port artificiel d'Arromanches au massacre de la prison de Caen, le matin même du Débarquement, retrouvez les fantômes qui hantent aujourd'hui encore Port-Winston.

UNE PLAGE EN ENFER
Omaha Beach - 6 juin 1944

- Patrick BOUSQUET-SCHNEEWEIS et Michel GIARD
- Format : 130 x 210 mm
- 80 pages intérieures
- Couverture souple
- Dos carré, collé, cousu
- Langues : français, anglais
- Prix : 7,50 €

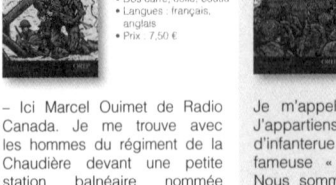

Je m'appelle William Bishop. J'appartiens à la 1re division d'infanterie américaine, la fameuse « Big Red One ». Nous sommes le 6 juin 1944 et, dans quelques minutes, je vais débarquer sur la plage d'Omaha la sanglante... Voici mon histoire...

LES ÉTOILES DE LA LIBERTÉ
Utah Beach - 6 juin 1944

- Patrick BOUSQUET-SCHNEEWEIS et Michel GIARD
- Format : 130 x 210 mm
- 80 pages intérieures
- Couverture souple
- Dos carré, collé, cousu
- Langues : français, anglais
- Prix : 7,50 €

Slapton Sands ! Une plage anglaise de sinistre mémoire pour tous ceux qui, comme le capitaine Schroeder, en avril 1944, avaient participé à l'opération *Tiger*, la tragique répétition du débarquement en Normandie.
Deux mois plus tard, à Utah Beach, Schroeder et ses hommes étaient bien décidés à venger la mort de leurs camarades...

À travers l'histoire de Leonard Schroeder, suivez l'épopée des soldats américains qui, le 6 juin 1944, ont recouvert les ténèbres de cinq années d'occupation sous une myriade d'étoiles. Les étoiles de la Liberté...

GO ! GERONIMO !
Sainte-Mère-Église - 6 juin 1944

- Patrick BOUSQUET-SCHNEEWEIS et Michel GIARD
- Format : 130 x 210 mm
- 80 pages intérieures
- Couverture souple
- Dos carré, collé, cousu
- Langues : français, anglais
- Prix : 7,50 €

« Steve, qui devait être le premier à franchir la porte du C-47, sentit son cœur battre la chamade. Cette fois, il n'était plus question de reculer.
– Go !, fit le largueur en lui tapant sur l'épaule.
– Geronimo !, s'écria Barrow en plongeant dans le vide obscur de la nuit.
Très vite, le ciel de Normandie se constella de centaines de corolles... »

Revivez la formidable épopée des paras de la 82e aéroportée qui sautèrent sur Sainte-Mère-Église dans la nuit du 5 au 6 juin 1944...

In the same collection

THE BLOODY MAPLES
Juno Beach - June 6th 1944

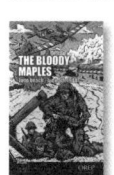

- Patrick BOUSQUET-SCHNEEWEIS and Michel GIARD
- Format: 130 x 210mm
- 80 inside pages
- Soft cover
- Square back, sewn, pasted
- Language: French, English
- Retail price: €7,50

– 'Marcel Ouimet from Radio Canada here. I am with men from the Régiment de La Chaudière in the small seaside resort of Bernières-sur-Mer. Shellfire from the German artillery batteries is intensifying all around us! The order is finally given to attack!
I can imagine the emotion felt by our troops during these historic moments, for many of them have French blood in them…'

From Montreal to Juno Beach, the incredible Canadian odyssey which, on the 6th of June 1944, contributed towards our newfound freedom...

THE GHOSTS OF PORT-WINSTON
Arromanches - June 6th 1944

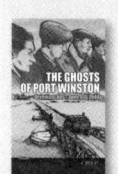

- Patrick BOUSQUET-SCHNEEWEIS and Michel GIARD
- Format: 130 x 210mm
- 80 inside pages
- Soft cover
- Square back, sewn, pasted
- Language: French, English
- Retail price: €7,50

The image of the ruins of Arromanches' artificial port brought tears to Julie's eyes and she began to shudder involuntarily. The ghosts she thought she had exorcised by coming here had returned. And she felt their presence stronger than ever…

From the construction of Arromanches' artificial port to the Caen prison massacre on the morning of D-Day, meet the ghosts which continue to haunt Port Winston today.

THE BEACH TO HELL
Omaha Beach - June 6th 1944

- Patrick BOUSQUET-SCHNEEWEIS and Michel GIARD
- Format: 130 x 210mm
- 80 inside pages
- Soft cover
- Square back, sewn, pasted
- Language: French, English
- Retail price: €7,50

My name is William Bishop. I belong to the US 1st Infantry Division, the famous Big Red One.
Today is the 6th of June 1944 and, in a few minutes, I'll be landing on Omaha Beach, in the Easy Red sector.
A beach that will go down in History as Bloody Omaha...
This is my story...

THE STARS OF LIBERTY
Utah Beach - June 6th 1944

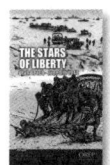

- Patrick BOUSQUET-SCHNEEWEIS and Michel GIARD
- Format: 130 x 210mm
- 80 inside pages
- Soft cover
- Square back, sewn, pasted
- Language: French, English
- Retail price: €7,50

Slapton Sands! The English beach holds dark memories for those who, like Captain Schroeder, took part in operation *Tiger* in April 1944, the rehearsal of the Normandy landings which ended in tragedy.
Two months later, on Utah Beach, Schroeder and his men are determined to avenge the death of their fellow soldiers…

Through Leonard Schroeder's story, follow the journey of American soldiers who, on the 6th of June 1944, put an end to the darkness of five years of occupation with a sea of stars. The stars of Liberty…

GO! GERONIMO!
Sainte-Mère-Église - June 6th 1944

- Patrick BOUSQUET-SCHNEEWEIS and Michel GIARD
- Format: 130 x 210mm
- 80 inside pages
- Soft cover
- Square back, sewn, pasted
- Language: French, English
- Retail price: €7,50

"Steve, who was to be the first to jump through the door of the C-47, could feel his heart beating like a drum. No danger of turning back this time.
"Go!" the dispatcher yelled as he tapped him on the shoulder.
"Geronimo!" cried Barrow as he plunged into the dark of the night.
The Normandy skies were soon to be illuminated by hundreds of garlands..."
Relive the epic feat of the 82nd Airborne paratroopers who jumped out over Sainte-Mère-Église on the night of the 5th to the 6th of June 1944...

Photographic credits

Cover illustrations: Arnaud Gaumet
p.58: Map by CRHQ
p.59: Maps by Yann Magdelaine
p.61: *Life Magazine*
p.60, 61, 63, 67, 68: Michel Giard collection
p.65: Map by OREP Éditions

ISBN : 978-2-8151-0181-3
© Éditions OREP 2014
All right reserved – **Legal Deposit:** 2nd quarter 2014